PhaithBook

A Compilation of Life-Changing Stories and Stats

Phaedra T. Anderson

ISBN: 978-0-9915202-4-4
First Edition Printing

Printed In the United States of America

March 2015

ChosenButterfly Publishing
P.O. Box 515
Millville, NJ 08332
www.cb-publishing.com

Table of Contents

Chapter 1: Phaith for the Journey

Chapter 2: Keeping it Simple

Chapter 3: The Woman in the Mirror

Chapter 4: You Glow Girl

This book is dedicated to the glory of God and to women all over the world.

Why PhaithBook?

PhaithBook was birthed during one of the darkest moments of my life. After being with a company for ten years, I was laid off. Laid off during a period of time when the world was facing a great recession that left millions of people unemployed and unable to find suitable employment. During this period many people lost their homes, their cars, and their life's savings. Poverty and homelessness were at an all-time high and there I was left unemployed for almost four years!

All I had was my faith. Faith that GOD would sustain me. Faith that GOD would provide for me. Faith that GOD would do what HE said that HE would do and that faith came from hearing HIS word and from being in HIS presence. The more GOD downloaded in me, the more I was able to download into others on social networks, such as Facebook. As I faced difficult situations in my life; I questioned how I was going to eat? How I was going to pay my bills? How I was going to survive? If I should marry? Should I stay? Should I leave? Should I go back to school? GOD would minister to me and give me words that would direct my path; that increased my faith, that gave me hope and that strengthened me. HE gave me words that gave me discernment; that opened my eyes and that increased wisdom in me. I in turn would put those words into parables, into articles and into text messages to share with my girlfriends and others.

After three years of writing what I thought to be just stats and stories to encourage myself; GOD instructed me to gather all of the material that I had posted on social networks, put it in a book and title it "**PhaithBook**".

PhaithBook is not only a girlfriend devotional - it is also a testament of my faith. A faith in Christ Jesus that got me through the unforeseen dark times. A faith that caused me to discover untapped resources during a time of lack. A faith that allowed me to know the strength that lay deep within me in order to handle what I thought to be unbearable. A faith that delivered me from the traps and snares of the enemy and that saved my life. This faith - Phaedra's faith, I share with you now in **PhaithBook**. I believe this book is filled with words that will give you hope, joy and peace. I also believe it will ultimately increase your faith in God - as well as in yourself, to be all that GOD created you to be no matter what you are currently going through. #DevelopedInDarkness
Be blessed!

Acknowledgements

I just want to take time to first thank **Jesus Christ my Lord and Savior,** because without HIM I can do nothing - but with HIM the sky is the limit. I truly thank GOD for trusting me with this precious gift of writing and exhortation and it is my prayer that I am using it in a way that makes HIM smile.

I thank **my Mom** for never allowing me to just be average. I thank my **Grandmother, the Late Ruth Mimms,** for passing me her writing baton. I thank **my God-father** and **all of the men at Graterford prison,** for they were my very first audience that supported me and encouraged me as a little girl to never dull my pencil.

Special thanks to **my cousin Nicky (Cole)** and to **my 'Bestie', Dahmiyah (Mi-Mi)** for always being the first to read my material, regardless of what time of the hour I submitted it....lol.

Thanks to **Alamo** for being my biggest fan and for pushing me to not sit on my gift and for believing in me when I didn't believe in myself.

I also want to thank **Ms. Shawn Chavis,** Editor-in-Chief of *Bronze Magazine,* **Dr. Cheryl Stuart,** Editor-in-Chief of Women of *Significance Magazine,* and Radio Show host, **Ms. Afi Pittman** for sharing your various platforms with me and for allowing my voice to be heard. You ladies are extraordinary and are the epitome of sisterhood.

I so appreciate my Publisher, **Pastor Ayanna Moore,** for being a God-send on so many different levels. I truly appreciate you for helping make my dream come true and bringing my baby to life.

A special, special thanks to **all of my Facebook friends** for your support and for your many words of encouragement - and thanks a million, to everyone that counted it not robbery to purchase this book. I truly appreciate you and I pray that you will read something that will make your today better than your yesterday.

Phaedra

xi

Foreword

If you are like me, you are one who absolutely loves wisdom, truth, encouragement and correction. If you like to hear or read messages that make you stop and think, you don't have to look any further! This book is filled with all of the above and so much more. I have been blessed to read many of the things that Phaedra has written along the years and they have made me laugh, think, shake my head and say "Girl, I know what you are talking about!" I was pleased and honored to be able to put her words to print so that many others could be blessed as well.

One of the many things I love about Phaedra's writing is the realness and truth within it. She has no problem telling others about where she has been, how she was able to come out, and where she is going, as long as it will encourage someone and bring glory to the Lord. It is people like her that we all need in our life because they help us to know what we are going through or feeling is not unusual. We ain't crazy and yes, if we hold onto the Lord's unchanging hand, things WILL get better after while!

I could go on and on about this book but since you have the book in your hand, read it and see for yourself. I was blessed and believe you will be too!

Enjoy,

Ayanna Moore
Publisher & CEO ChosenButterfly Publishing
www.cb-publishing.com

~Sister~

Sis, time waits for no one

No! Not even you

So, you must be aware of the things that you do

You're no longer a baby

You're a woman now

So it's time to get out there and face life's ups and downs

It's time get out there on the field

You either win or you lose; the word of GOD is your shield

Sister, the winds of life are strong and they'll blow you in any direction

Only the strong stand still and failure has no selection

Your experiences and mistakes you must take heed to and learn from them

Only you can conquer your fears in life

Only you can overcome them

Every day that you live there's a lesson to be learned

Open your mind and acquire the wisdom that you've earned

Never doubt yourself and say that you "can't"

Because, if you thought that you could then there's a chance that you can

Always be independent and do for yourself

Never love no man more than you love yourself

Never settle for less when you deserve the best

And never lower GOD'S standards just to please the rest

Never play second field when your place is on a throne

Sis, you are a QUEEN never take the position as a pawn

Listen, when HE speaks

HE'LL never leave you astray
HE'S that little voice in your heart that you
sometimes turn away
HE'S your protector
Your spiritual guide
HE'S that feeling that you get when something just isn't right
Sis, it's HIM
Mistake Him for none other
In times of need HE'LL be your sister, your mother
HE can provide you with all the love that you need
For HE is the Holy Spirit and in you is HE
Sister

Chapter 1
Phaith for the Journey

Against All Odds.....

One of my sisters shared a photo with me and it immediately spoke volumes to me. As I looked at it, my creative juices started to flow. My mind started to race as the tears began to fall, because this picture reminded me so much of myself. As I stared at that rose, all I could see was a little girl growing up in an environment that was not conducive for life to grow in; an environment that was not cultivated with nourishment, but designed to smother dreams and possibilities. An environment that so many young women grow up in and have to fight their way through.

But just like that rose, we push through those hard places in life. We fight through the oppositions, break the boundaries and blossom against all odds, because when God has predestined you to be, to do and to go - there isn't an environment dire enough to stop the plan of God. When you are a child of destiny and purpose - you flourish, you bloom, you blossom and you come forth, even in hard places. So it doesn't matter if you were planted in a healthy environment or an unhealthy environment. You blossom right where you are, because as the song says, "A ROSE is STILL and will ALWAYS be a ROSE", even if it has to GROW against all odds.

NOTHING CAN HOLD A GOOD ROSE DOWN!

The Storm Is Almost Over...

A category five storm is the strongest and most severe class of hurricanes on the measuring scale for hurricane strength. The intensity of the winds and floods are capable of causing complete roof failure on buildings, coastal damage and city flooding. That was the result of Hurricane Katrina. Those that survived Hurricane Katrina were saved by the love of God and nothing else. For nothing but God was able to keep them in the days of trouble; serving as their strong tower, hiding them under His wings of protection, keeping them grounded while everything and everyone around them were blown away. Nobody but God was able to sustain them through floods and winds of that magnitude. Nobody but God was able to restore back to them all that was damaged by the winds and destroyed by the flood.

My sister - you too are a category 5 SURVIVOR, which is why you must always remember the strength that lies within you. Don't let depression, defeat, or discouragement get the best of you. Your category 5 survival skills have already been proven. If you have lived through the loss of a mother, father, or a child - then you are a category-5 SURVIVOR. If you have been through a divorce, lay-off, or sickness - then you are a category-5 SURVIVOR. If you have overcome an addiction or recovered after a house fire - then you are a category-5 SURVIVOR, for you have already survived a category-5 storm. So don't ever let the enemy make you think that you don't have what it takes to make it through a category 1, 2, or 3 storm. You are a category-5 SURVIVOR and the same GOD that got you through the hurricane is the same GOD that will get you through the storm. So rejoice, because this too shall pass. The storm is almost over and you will be restored!

Back In The Game....

Since I was 8 years old, I said that I would write a book. After high school, I had plans to attend college and have my degree by the time I was 21. At 25, I set a goal to own my first house by the time I was 30 - but at 33, I have yet to accomplish any of these goals because as you know, sometimes life doesn't go exactly as we plan. Things happen, families happen, children happen, bills happen, layoffs happen, distractions happen and somewhere down the line while 'life is happening'; our dreams get delayed, our vision becomes distorted, our plans are misplaced and the MVP gets knocked out of his own game and plays the sideline.

I played the sideline for years, mainly because I had allowed fear to tell me that *'I was too old and that it was too late for me to get back in my own game.'* I had allowed fear to tell me that *'I couldn't do it and that I wouldn't be successful at it if I did.'* That paralyzed me, causing me to get stuck on the bench; scared to get back in the game, scared to pick up the ball and scared to take a shot. But as I continued attending church and hearing the Word of God, my faith started to supersede my fears and after a job lay off, I found myself back in the game.

Since I've been back in the game I've started my book and I'm six classes short of my degree. I'm also a certified massage therapist and nail technician - and in two months, I will have graduated from Jean Madeline Aveda Institute as an Esthetician, with plans to open my own business. Although I have yet to meet my goals 100%, the MVP is no longer on the sideline and I have a far greater chance of winning on the court than I did on the bench. You have to at least be in the game in order to win the game - and if I can get back in the game, so can you.

What we must understand is that age is not a deterrent or an obstacle to God; so if fear is telling you that 'It's too late' or 'It's not going to work because you are too old', the Lord says: *"Thou art old and stricken in years, and there remaineth yet very much land to be possessed"* (Joshua 13:1). So no matter what age you are, re-visit your game plan; write the vision, pursue your dream, open your business, write your book, sing your song, get that degree, patent that idea, start that ministry and GET BACK IN THE GAME!

The ball is in your court. Now dunk it, because I am!

I can do all things through Christ who strengtheneth me.

(Philippians 4:13)

Developed In Darkness.....

I am not exactly sure where you are in your life, but I can give you a brief summary of where I am. I am in what appears to be the darkest hour of my life. I feel as if I am living life with my eyes closed and I can't see anything around me. It is as if God has placed me in a darkroom with the door closed and my only instructions are to 'WAIT AND LISTEN' because if I come out too soon, I will be distorted and if I go by what I see, I will become confused, because what I am seeing and what I am hearing are not one in the same.

In the dark, I see that my unemployment has stopped. I see that my bills are due. I see that I am trying to start a business and write a book with limited resources and space. I see that I don't have any health benefits. I see that my money is real funny. However I hear, "Your God shall supply all of your needs according to His riches in Glory by Christ Jesus". I hear, "You can do all things through Christ Jesus who strengthens you." I hear, "Blessed the Lord, Oh my soul and forget not all His benefits." I hear, "It is the Lord, thy God that gives you power to produce wealth." So as you see, what I see and what I hear are complete opposites and although both are realities - I have chosen to lean on what I hear and wait on HIS WORD, because God is not a man that He should lie and if He said it, He will make it good.

So while I continue to wait in this darkroom, I have a feeling that I am not alone. There are others waiting in this darkroom too and I come to encourage you today because this is just the development process. Negatives are always developed in darkrooms and it is in these rooms where GOD is doing some of His best work. It is in this place where GOD is perfecting you. It is in this place where GOD is establishing you. It is in this place where GOD is developing you. It is in these darkrooms where we transform from negatives that no one is able to make out, to beautiful pictures that bring GOD GLORY!

Be encouraged in your darkroom because you are coming out as a PERFECT PICTURE.

Close Your Ears!

When Jesus died on the cross, He died for all of our sins. Once we accept Him into our lives as our LORD and SAVIOR, we are forgiven. *"If we confess our sins, He is faithful and just to forgive us our sins and to cleanse us from all unrighteousness"* (1 John 1:9). But the enemy attempts to remind us of our sins and tries to make us believe we are not forgiven, which causes us to walk in guilt, shame and condemnation. However today, I declare and decree that you are free from guilt and condemnation, because JESUS died so that you may live and that you may be forgiven.

So CLOSE YOUR EARS to the ACCUSER and to his lies, because GOD has FORGIVEN you for the SIN. He has FORGIVEN you for the LIES. HE has FORGIVEN you for the DECEPTION. HE has FORGIVEN you for harboring HATRED, JEALOUSY AND ENVY. HE has FORGIVEN you for being DISOBEDIENT. HE has FORGIVEN you for the DIVORCE. HE has FORGIVEN you for the FORNICATION. HE has FORGIVEN you for being RUDE. HE has FORGIVEN you for GAMBLING. HE has FORGIVEN you for harboring UNFORGIVENESS. HE has FORGIVEN you for the ADULTERY. HE has FORGIVEN you of IDOLATRY. Once you have confessed your sins before God, it doesn't matter how you feel, you must believe and know that He has FORGIVEN you for ALL of those habitual acts that do not please HIM.

~ You are forgiven ~

"For the accuser of our brethren is cast down, which accused them before our God day and night" (Revelation 12:10).

Single, Saved & Loving God......

It's amazing how the world and at times, even the church may make you feel inadequate as a woman if you are not married by a certain age, but I remember a woman of God telling me years ago to enjoy my singlehood as long as I could. She was a married woman and she expressed to me that although she loved her husband and her family, she missed being in that secret place in GOD as a single woman. I must say that at the time I didn't understand her, but now things in my life are starting to change and I fully understand. For I now reside in that place and I see how those divided interests may be a challenge - especially for a woman that has been accustomed to devoting her time in the presence of God and doing the work of the Lord. Although there is nothing wrong with being married, for it is a beautiful thing - but there is much value, real joy and a gift in being a SINGLE WOMAN grounded in the LORD for...

"The unmarried woman careth for the things of the Lord, that she may be holy both in body and in spirit: but she that is married careth for the things of the world, how she may please her husband"
(1 Corinthians 7:34).

Waiting On God

Three of my friends felt that God was taking too long to move, to answer, or to come - so they went on and did things their way. They married who they wanted to marry. They had children with who they wanted to have children with. They purchased the homes that they wanted to purchase. They moved and took jobs where they wanted to live. They did all of this without knowing the WILL OF GOD for their lives and NOW some of them are divorced after a short time of being married. Some have children with people they don't even care to look at and now they have to spend the next 18 years of their lives dealing with a person they wish they never had to see again. Some have invested their entire life's savings in homes they no longer have and/or are struggling to keep and some have picked up and moved to other states for jobs that seemed right, only to have the company close in a few months.

So no matter how anxious, frustrated or annoyed I may become; no matter how weird or strange I may look and no matter how long I have to wait...I will be sitting right here...even if I have to sit alone...I will not MOVE until GOD'S will is revealed to me.

"I had fainted, unless I had believed to see the goodness of the Lord in the land of the living. Wait on the Lord: be of good courage, and He shall strengthen thine heart: wait, I say, on the Lord" (Psalm 27:13-14).

More Than Just A Temp

The economy is still uncertain. Healthcare requirements are still changing and companies are still playing it safe by not making long-term commitments to employees. So during this season while in between jobs and in between building our own empires, many of us will seek employment from temporary staffing agencies.

I know! Who would have thought that you would be working TEMPORARY ASSIGNMENTS at this stage in your life? But the truth of the matter is, you are! The one thing that you have to know and have embedded in your mind is that 'YOU ARE MORE THAN JUST A TEMP' and your attitude and your work productivity should reflect that. This especially goes for the child of God, because the moment that you walk into a building - you have to know that the company just got blessed. Why? Because you are there and wherever the presence of GOD is, it is blessed. Not only that, but do you know that you have been chosen, picked out and hand selected for that particular assignment? Out of all the candidates they could have selected, they chose YOU. So do your job with excellence. You never know what may come out of it and you never know who might be watching you.

I got called for a 30-day temp assignment making $12 an hour and it turned into a 10-year permanent position; making over $60,000 a year with two company credit cards, perks and full benefits - and that was without a degree. So change your perspective. Wear professional attire. Have a pleasant attitude. Work with pride and put a smile on your face, because YOU ARE MORE THAN JUST A TEMP. You are a SERVANT OF THE MOST HIGH GOD sent on a TEMPORARY ASSIGNMENT to make a PERMANENT IMPRESSION.

Boundaries: Stick To The Script

Boundary: Any line or thing marking a limit;
Bound; border

We set boundaries in our lives as defense mechanisms; to protect ourselves from unwanted people and situations. But how many of us draw these lines which represent our beliefs, standards, morals, values and so forth - only to find that we allow people to continuously cross them, go against them, insult them and violate them? We allow others to step way beyond their boundaries and overstay their welcome. Far too often - we compromise, conform to the needs of others and become people-pleasers. Slowly but surely, we begin to lose ourselves - along with everything that we stood for in the process. Things that we vowed we would never stand for and that we would never do, start to become a part of our everyday lives but at some point, we must draw the line. We must stick to the script and say, "This is what I will and will not tolerate."

When a director is directing a movie and an actor or actress is having problems with the script and experiencing difficulty playing the role of that specific character - the director doesn't change the script to please the actor or actress, but instead he replaces the actor or actress with one that is more fitting for the part.

He knows that if he were to change the script, the movie would be altered and the outcome would be different from what the writer intended.

You are the WRITER, the DIRECTOR and the STAR of the movie called 'YOUR LIFE' and you get to select your ALL-STAR CAST. You decide which characters have leading roles and which characters are supporting actors. You decide which characters get to stay and which characters die off. Don't let anyone cross their boundaries and alter your movie.

Lego My Ego

A few years ago, I gave my life to Christ and shortly after, I noticed that I had begun doing some things that were strange to me. For instance, I was forgiving people that had hurt me. I was holding my tongue instead of lashing out. I was walking away instead of arguing my point. I was praying for people that I knew didn't like me. I was helping people even though they remained unappreciative. I was speaking to people even if they didn't speak to me first. I was allowing people to pass me after they had cut me off while driving. I even started apologizing to people even when the offense wasn't on me and often this was a struggle, because my ego told me that I was becoming weak: I was allowing people to disrespect me. My ego was telling me that I was beginning to allow people to take advantage of me and shortly, they would start taking my kindness for weakness.

The closer I got to God, the more my ego was challenged and I would often have to make the decision to please God or to please my ego. My ego was the way that I perceived myself; who I believed I was, how I believed I was supposed to respond to people, things and situations - and of course, how they were to respond to me. My ego was my identity, my will … what I believed about myself that made me important and strong. The more I studied the Word of God, the more I learned that my ego had nothing to do with God's will for my life. I actually started to realize that my ego wasn't me at all. It had somehow stolen my identity and had become a major distraction in my life and was retarding my growth in various areas.

There was too much 'I and me' and not enough Him (God). My ego was a false sense of myself and it caused me to be prideful, selfish, self-centered, arrogant, uncompassionate, judgmental, rebellious and combative. As long as I fed it, it made me feel important, respected and powerful. My ego wouldn't dare allow someone to verbally disrespect me without my responding back in the same manner - although Proverbs 15:1 says, *"A soft answer turneth away wrath: but grievous words stir up anger"*.

I had subconsciously made my ego my god, because I had allowed it to be the deciding factor in my life. It meant more to me to please it, than to please God and we serve a jealous God. He will not tolerate us worshiping or bowing down to any other god other than Him (Exodus 20:4-6). So when my ego met the Holy Spirit, it began to lose its power, because: *"For the word of God is quick, and powerful, and sharper than any two edged sword, piercing even to the dividing asunder of soul and spirit, and of the joints and marrow, and is a discerner of the thoughts and intents of the heart"* (Hebrews 4:12). As my ego started to die, the God in me started to live and slowly but surely, I began to LEGO MY EGO and get my identity back. Now the REAL ME is finally able to shine.

Stand Up

The main causes of identity theft are ALTER EGOS, SUPERFICIAL IMAGES and PRETENTIOUS ATTITUDES. If you KILL the EGO, LOSE the IMAGE and GET RID of the ATTITUDE, you will FIND YOURSELF and get your IDENTITY BACK. So KNOCKOUT your EGO today, so that the REAL YOU can STAND UP.

The Coward In Me

A few weeks ago, I offended one of my sisters in Christ by exiting my responsibilities without giving her proper notice. I literally abandoned my position, which was ungodly - for we are to do all things with decency and in order. I lost peace over it because I knew I was wrong and had now become a source of someone else's pain. I found myself avoiding her and not wanting to answer her calls, because I don't like conflict and just wasn't ready to face her; although I knew that one day soon I would have to clean up the mess I had now made. This was a blow to my character and integrity and that just didn't sit well with me.

I would see her number appear on my caller ID and it actually made me nervous, so I just didn't answer. But one day while in prayer, it was as if God had put His hands over His ears and said, *"I don't want to hear anything that you have to say, until you get things right with your sister."* So that morning I called her, but the COWARD in me called during a time that I knew she wouldn't be there. I left a message with an apology, but the CHRISTIAN in me knew that I was still out of order because she deserved a verbal apology. So I called again at a time that I knew that she would be at her place of business and apologized. The woman of God forgave me and released me in prayer. I thank God for that because as children of God, we are called to be more than CONQUERORS - not COWARDS and when we offend someone, it is our responsibility to make it right with that person.

Don't let fear rule you and don't allow the COWARD IN YOU to live another day. If you have offended anyone, make it your business to reconcile things with them today and put the COWARD in you to death. I did and I must say that it feels a lot better being a CONQUEROR.

"Let all things be done decently and in order" (1 Corinthians 14:40).

Got Fruit?

Maturity is a must in order for the believer to develop into the full stature of the man or woman that God has called one to be. God is concerned about each of us GROWING UP. HE expects us to GROW UP in HIM, but far too often we remain BABIES. We remain carnal and never grow in the wisdom and knowledge that God has made available to us. Many of us never perfect our ministries and never produce any fruits of the Spirit in our lives, simply because we refuse to GROW UP. GROWING up in God is much more than saying that I have a title or a ministry or saying that I've been saved for a number of years, because that doesn't necessarily prove growth.

The proof of GROWTH and MATURITY in God is your FRUIT. It is impossible for anyone to GROW in the knowledge and the grace of God and NOT produce any FRUIT in their lives. So check your tree and see if you have any fruit and by that - determine how GROWN you really are or how much GROWING up you need to do. *"But the fruit of the Spirit is love, joy, peace, longsuffering, gentleness, goodness, faith, meekness, temperance: against such there is no law"* (Galatians 5:22-23). #GrowUp

The Gucci Bag Lady

As I watched the GUCCI BAG LADY dig in her bag to get her keys, I noticed that it took her every bit of five minutes just to find them. Thank God she wasn't being chased, because she would have gotten caught. I thought wow, she must have a lot of junk in her bag. I mean she must have to dig through her eyeglass case, wallet, make-up compact, receipts, mail envelopes, church bulletins, tissues, flyers, invitations and several other unnecessary items just to find the one thing she needed - her keys.

As I watched her put her keys in the door, I couldn't help but wonder: is her pocketbook subliminal to her life? Does she carry around a bunch of unwanted, unnecessary stuff that makes it difficult for her to get to the things she really needs? Does she arrive late to places because she has so much excessive baggage slowing her down? I even started to wonder if everything in her bag actually belonged to her. She probably doesn't even notice that the weight on her shoulders would be so much lighter if she would just stop carrying around other people's baggage.

After that day, I was never able to look at the GUCCI BAG LADY the same because even though from the outside she looked sophisticated, luxurious and well-put together - on the inside, she was unorganized, cluttered and weighted down. No matter what tag or label you put on it - whether FENDI, BURBERRY, MARC JACOB, LOUIS VUITTON or CHANEL, there's nothing pretty or attractive about baggage. So after that day, I went home and cleaned out my pocketbooks because I didn't want to be the GUCCI BAG LADY anymore.

No More Counterfeits!

A Multi-Function Counterfeit Money Detection Machine is designed to detect the authenticity of bills, credit cards, traveler's checks and other special documents using different devices. Well, as a believer and as a DAUGHTER OF THE MOST HIGH GOD, you too have a Multi-Function Counterfeit Detector in you and HE'S called the HOLY GHOST. Amongst a host of other things, He is well able to help you detect the authenticity of any man that may come across your path: from the whoremonger to the user, to the drama king, to the bum, to the distractor, to the church playboy - down to the man of God. So spend time with Him and He will begin to heighten your spiritual discernment. You will be able to see the real from the fake a mile away.

Got Favor?

Have you ever been in the super market with long checkout lines and as soon as you walk up, a new line opens? Have you ever lost your wallet and had someone mail it to your house with all of your belongings still in it? Have you ever left your cell phone in a store only to find that someone turned it in to the lost and found? Have you even gotten a job that you weren't qualified for? If so, that's favor and there's nothing like the favor that God bestows on His children.

I'll never forget the first time that I learned about the favor of God. I was working for a temp agency in 1999. I got called for an assignment that was only supposed to last for 30 days. In 2004, I was offered the position as a permanent employee. But here's the kicker: in 2002, the company had undergone major organizational changes which included the elimination of my position and everyone - including my boss, knew that my position had been eliminated. So for two years I worked at a job that didn't even exist and what was supposed to be a 30-day assignment, turned into a ten-year position. Often people would ask me questions like, "How were you able to be a temp for that long?" and "How did you get that job without a degree?" My response would always be, "It's the favor of God." So as you can see, favor can open doors that normally wouldn't be open to the child of God and it also causes seeing eyes to not see.

Favor is also the extension of God's grace and salvation of man. God sent Jesus Christ to save us even when we were not worthy of that salvation. If that isn't an undeserving privilege, then I don't know what is. For while we were yet sinners, unfit and unworthy - God still had special regard for His children. He demonstrated His love for us by dying on the cross. Now eternal life is our gift and there's nothing that we had to do or could have done in order to earn or obtain this favor from God. All we have to do is accept it. Who wouldn't accept a favor from God? And once the favor of salvation is received, unmerited favor encircles the life of the believer. I can tell you that this favor will put you in front of the right people - at the right time and saying the right things, because with the favor of God comes the wisdom of God.

There are so many benefits that the child of God can experience when they have the favor of God. If you are still unsure as to what favor is, it's you picking up a check from your lawyer and he says, "As a courtesy to you, I've reduced your legal fees, so that you could have more money." Favor is finding a house that exceeded your budget, only to find it still on the market a year later at a reduced price just for you. Favor is an added benefit to the child of God that walks in obedience. Favor is peace, joy, victory, freedom and mercy. There's nothing like having the favor of God. Now that you know exactly what the favor of God is, look back on your life and ask yourself, "GOT FAVOR?"

Chapter 2

Keeping It Simple...

The teaching of your word gives light, so even the simple can understand (Psalm 119:130 - NLT).

~ Don't be so deep when you teach that you can't reach ~

The Process

When we FIRST come to CHRIST, we come as we are with all of our junk. HE accepts us with all of our trash and with all of the trash that others have dumped in our lives, in our minds, in our souls and in our spirits - but HE doesn't expect for us to stay that way. So after listening to HIS WORD, we start to change a little but not too much, because the seed is still falling on fallow ground. So the HOLY GHOST starts to break up the fallow ground, rakes the weeds and removes the debris and trash that's preventing the seeds from growing. Then we start to work with the WORD and we begin cleaning up the areas in our lives that we have control over.

We start fasting, praying, spending time in prayer, delivering up praise and worship and reading the Word - because now we are able to see that it's a joint effort. We clean up what we can clean up on the surface and GOD cleans up what HE needs to clean up from the roots. Now, the soil is clear; healing, forgiveness, brokenness, purification, sanctification, etc. has taken place and now our spirits, minds and souls are clean.

FINALLY, the anointing can flow with ease through our lives and our gardens are now ready to produce for the glory of GOD.

~ IT'S A PROCESS, BUT IT'S WORTH IT ~

Too Small Shoes

Have you ever tried on a pair of shoes that were a bit tight and maybe even too small for you, but you were so fond of them that you purchased them anyway? You just had to have them. You were so into the look of the shoe that you totally disregarded the pain they would cause to your feet, figuring it wouldn't be that bad. Suppressing the fact that you already know from the beginning that you can't fit those shoes, you buy them anyway. So, you wore them the first time and there was some discomfort - but you figured you would stretch them out, change the shape a little, so that they would fit you. You wear them a second time and you still notice some discomfort, but it's still bearable.

However, once you take them off you notice that there's a cut on your foot where the material started to rub your skin off, but you like the shoes so much, you wear them again and this time they kill you. You've walked in them for so long that it feels like your feet are bleeding. They start to affect your walk, your balance and your back. Your feet now have calluses and blisters and the pain is so unbearable that you are forced to take them off. At this point you begin to curse those stupid shoes, but the shoes are just fine. Actually, the shoes were perfect. They just weren't for you. You have now inflicted pain upon yourself, because you thought that you could change the size and shape of a shoe that was not made for you.

My point is, a lot of times we try to make ourselves fit in places where we know we don't belong or force ourselves onto people who we know we don't belong with. Did you ever stop to think that maybe that person is rejecting you - not because they don't care, but maybe he/she is not equipped to handle a person of your caliber? Just like that shoe was not made to fit a foot your size? Sometimes we try to force ourselves onto people and GOD has not equipped that person to carry us; God has not given that person the gifts to add to the joy and happiness in our lives. Often we continue to force it, because we are so infatuated with a look and we end up crippling ourselves in the process, because the more we force it - the more pain it causes us, until finally we are so bruised and beaten, drained and unstable that we have no choice but to let that person go.

GOD has given us all a spirit that signals us from the very beginning when something is not for us. It's time we start to listen and stop trying to get in where we don't fit in, so that we can live up to HIS standards and walk in the shoes that HE has made for us; so that our walk is in peace, our walk is straight and with integrity, grace and righteousness.

Iron Out the Wrinkles

Just like we take the time to iron out the wrinkles in our clothes before we put them on, we should take the same time and consideration to iron out some issues in our relationships before we get married. Imagine how uncomfortable and painful it would be to have someone iron your clothes while you were wearing them. That's how uncomfortable and painful it is to iron out some issues after getting married.

So don't be in a rush. Take your time and use the courting/dating process to lay all your issues on the ironing board and apply as much heat as needed to get those wrinkles out. For once you put that marriage outfit on, there is no taking it off and you want it to be as wrinkle-free as possible. Now you may not get every wrinkle out, but it sure makes sense to IRON OUT as much as you can!

Get Off The See-Saw

Many of us are unstable and can't make concrete decisions. One minute we love them and the next minute, we don't. One minute, we are dieting, the next minute we are not. One minute, we are in church loving Jesus, the next - we are in the world shaking our tail feather. I have found that we are up and down in the minor things in life, because we are up and down and have no loyalty in the MAJOR things in life. *"Their loyalty is divided between God and the world, and they are unstable in everything they do"* (James 1:8).

~ You will NEVER be stable. You will always be wishy-washy
until you get stable in GOD. ~

Gird 'Em Up, Girl!

Roman soldiers during the Bible days wore long, flowing robes but when they went out to battle, the robes were tied between their legs so that they could be as mobile as possible, preventing them from falling. If the robe wasn't tied up, it would hinder them from moving swiftly and being strong enough to fight. Today the LORD is saying to HIS soldiers, *"GIRD UP YOUR LOINS. GET DRESSED FOR BATTLE. CLEAR YOUR MIND AND MAKE YOURSELF AS STRONG AND VIGOROUS AS POSSIBLE. BE PREPARED TO PUT FORTH THE HIGHEST EFFORT, BECAUSE THE TASK THAT GOD IS ABOUT TO PUT YOU TO WILL REQUIRE ALL OF YOUR ABILITY!"* The enemy will use any source to hinder your walk with the Lord, starting with your thoughts. So focus your thoughts on those things that will allow you to serve God successfully and eliminate any tie between your legs, any thoughts, things or people that may trip you up and cause you to stumble during battle.

~ BRACE YOURSELF ~

I'm In Love With a Stripper!

The more I stay in GOD'S PRESENCE, the more HIS LOVE strips the old shellac and varnish from my life. Overtime, the shellac and varnish have made me darken, dull and have hidden my natural beauty. HIS stripping process is so thorough, that it strips me without harming me as it sands through my build-ups, buffs and shines me at the same time. LOVE strips, buffs and shines you back to your natural self and reveals you anew.

#StrippedDown2Perfection

Closed Doors

I don't know about you, but I have to close the door on some things. I have to close the door of my past; the door of fear, the door of procrastination, the door of forgetfulness and the door of poverty. I have to close some doors my flesh has opened. I have to close some doors that my ancestors have opened. I have to close these doors! LORD, help me to close these doors, because I can't afford to miss the doors that you open for me!

#closingthedoorontheenemy

You're Sexy & You Know It!

Somebody told us that wearing tight clothing makes us SEXY. Someone also told us that the fewer clothes we wear, the sexier we look. I'm here to tell you that they *lied,* because I see women every day that are half-naked and NOTHING about them says 'SEXY'. Everything about them says 'I've been HURT, REJECTED, VIOLATED, ABANDONED and NOW I DON'T KNOW WHO I AM' because SEXY isn't based on what you have on you. It's more so predicated on what you have in you and it's NOT something that you TRY to be. It's something that you just are and most times, we try too hard and we wear too less, because you can have on a burlap sack and still be SEXY. For if you are SEXY and YOU KNOW IT, you don't have to BARE IT ALL TO SHOW IT!

Does He Still Love Me?

I SERVED ANOTHER god. DOES JESUS STILL LOVE ME?

I remember a time in my younger years when I denied Christ and chose to follow another god. Once I gave my life to Christ, the enemy would remind me of the time that I denied JESUS as my LORD and Savior and he would tell me that I wasn't forgiven and that I wasn't saved. I never shared those thoughts with anyone, but GOD knew my concerns and one day GOD took me to the BOOK of RUTH and made HIS forgiveness very plain to me.

RUTH was a Moabite and she served another god prior to being introduced to the GOD of the Hebrews. *"Now they took wives of the women of Moab: the name of the one was Orpah, and the name of the other Ruth"* (Ruth 1:4). History tells us that the Moabites were polytheists and that they served many gods. Chemosh, Ashtar and Nebo were a few of the gods that they served and they would perform sexual rituals and make human sacrifices to these gods, often killing children. These were the gods that RUTH served, until she met her husband and her mother-in-law, Naomi. Once her husband died, she never left her mother-in-law and vowed to serve her GOD: *"Where you go I will go and where you stay I will stay. Your people will be my people and your God my God"* (Ruth 1:16).

Ruth, later on would be the grandmother of KING DAVID. So not only was she forgiven, but GOD used her womb to birth DAVID and JESUS' mother MARY, was betrothed to JOSEPH of the lineage of DAVID and in Christian lineage - RUTH is a foremother of JESUS. Are you getting this? Ruth, who was a Moabite woman that served several gods was now a foremother of JESUS. Now how BIG is that?

And I tell you once GOD gave it to me like that, I never questioned if I was forgiven again - and you beloved, don't have to question it either. I don't care what god you may have served in the past, once you have repented from committing idolatry and once you have accepted JESUS as your LORD and SAVIOR, all of your sins are under the blood to be remembered no more and there's NOTHING that NOBODY can do about that.

So know that JESUS still loves you and is willing to forgive you and can still birth something great out of you.

Wash Me!

If we can be real for a minute, there are some areas in our lives that we struggle with. There are some areas of iniquity, sin or habits that aren't sinful, but aren't beneficial either. It's in those areas that we might need constant or repeated washings in order to remove those stains. I'm not talking about light stains that can be removed with one wipe: I'm talking about deep stains that have the ability to destroy our godly garments. I'm talking about stains that are so deep, that your great, great, great grandmother could have made them and here it is decades later and you're left struggling trying to get out generational stains such as; rebellion, addiction, lust, perversion, homosexuality, gambling, stealing, alcoholism, gossip, fornication, adultery, hatred, etc.

When it comes to these stains, sometimes one washing won't do. They require thorough, repeated, multiple washings and the sanctifying influences of the Holy Spirit in order to be removed for good. So if you know that I'm telling the truth about it and if you desire to be clean as well, join me as I take my soul to the Laundromat today and ask GOD to *"Wash me thoroughly from mine iniquity, and cleanse me from my sin"* (Psalm 51:2).

~ Where there is truth, GOD will give wisdom. ~

Chapter 3
The Woman In The Mirror

~ You can take the time to evaluate yourself or choose not to, but either way, somebody will. ~

To Thine Own Self Be True

I have to admit that never in a million years did I think that I would be quoting William Shakespeare. As a young African American woman from the urban streets of Philadelphia, better known as the "hood", Shakespeare was not taught in our schools. Edgar Allan Poe, Geoffrey Chaucer, Charles Dickens and the other great writers were not a part of our English curriculum. So I did not have the privilege of being exposed to Hamlet, which many identify as being the most famous play in the English language. However now at 30-something, as I embark on making some of the most critical decisions in my life - I now find myself intrigued by this great writer (Shakespeare) and I see this quote "To thine own self be true" as pivotal to my very existence.

"This above all" preceded the last advice that Polonius gave to his son Laertes, as he departed for Paris and he said to him, "This above all: to thine own self be true." As I read it, I immediately paused to look in the mirror and asked myself, "Have I been true to you?" Yes, I have been loyal to my friends, my family, and my career - but have I been loyal to myself? And the more I look at myself and engage in this intense self-reflection, I'm made to see all of the times where I've put on masks and took the center stage instead of being true to me. I'm rolling back all of the scenes where I said "Yes" only because I knew that someone else did not want to hear "No". I see flashbacks of times where I went 'there' when I really wanted to go 'there', times where I stayed in 'that' because I was too afraid to move into 'that' and then, there are those very unpleasant scenes where I just flat-out entered into self-deception and took the truth and exaggerated it to the point where I couldn't even tell that I was in a bad situation. That must have been the peak of my acting career, because I had manipulated the truth so much in those scenes that I actually made a few bad situations seem better than what they actually were. I contribute it all to not being true to myself.

So many times we find ourselves in unhappy situations, in bad marriages, in unfulfilled careers, in unfruitful affairs and it's not because of what someone else did to us, or because we were not presented with the facts. It's simply because we weren't being honest with ourselves in the very beginning when we made those decisions, when we said "yes" and accepted those offers. However just like this play, at some point the acting has to stop - the masks have to be removed, the play has to end and the curtains have to close. You have to go home, look yourself in the mirror and ask yourself, *"Above all else: Have I been true to you?*

Where are Your Shoes?

I didn't mind driving to Nordstrom at the Cherry Hill Mall on Monday to get my shoes because the drive was short - but when I arrived, they didn't have the shoes I wanted. The only other Nordstrom was at King of Prussia (mall) and I hate that drive; but on Monday they had a few pairs left and I really wanted those shoes, but not bad enough to drive those extra miles. So I took a gamble and said that I would wait until Tuesday. Once Tuesday came, I drove out to King of Prussia only to find that they didn't have my shoes out on display and it appeared that they didn't have any in stock.

I became disappointed and upset with myself because I really wanted those shoes, but I didn't want them bad enough to drive out there on Monday. Now it appeared that someone else had purchased the last pair and although I didn't see any out on display, I just had to ask the salesperson if they had any in stock. Thank God they had one pair in the back and they were the perfect color, fit and size. The salesperson informed me that they don't place shoe styles with only a few pairs in stock out on display. You have to ask for them and it made me think about how God is with HIS daughters. Because we are so rare and important to HIM, HE doesn't put us on display nor does HE want us putting ourselves on display for any man to try on for size. HE keeps us in the back, hidden under HIS wings and if a man desires to have one of HIS daughters, he has to take some extra steps. He has to do those things that he doesn't want to do. He has to give up those things that he doesn't want to give up in order to show God that he's serious and capable of caring for one of HIS precious daughters. He has to be willing to travel those extra miles in order to get to that place where God is in order to ask for her; then and only then does God lift HIS wings to reveal her, bring her from the back and release her to him in the perfect color, fit and size.

A wise woman once said, "A woman should be so hidden in GOD that a man has to seek GOD in order to find her." So my question to you today is, "Are your shoes hidden or are they on display?" **Where are your shoes?**

Are You Drowning?

I recall a time when shacking up was frowned upon. It used to be an uncommon thing to see an unmarried couple engaged in a sexual relationship and living together. This type of living arrangement used to be shameful for a woman and it brought embarrassment to her family; so much so, that if it were done, it had to be in secret.

Times have changed. And even though shacking up is acceptable in society and is pretty much the norm now for the world - GOD's word is still the same. Shacking up and fornication are still sins in the eyes of GOD, which leads me to ask these questions: "If you say that you are saved - but yet you have been shacking up with a man or a woman for one, two, five, ten or fifteen years, are you really saved? Or are you just a church goer? Do you still get convicted? Or has the Holy Spirit left you to yourself because you have grieved HIM so much with your disobedience and your rebellious attitude? Have you failed to listen to the Holy Spirit to the point that your heart is hardened and your ears are closed to His correction and pricking?"

I'm just asking because I see this lifestyle being adopted within the body of Christ and it makes me wonder. I have tried shacking up myself once upon a time and as a Christian woman, the conviction was so heavy that I had to throw that man out of my house. We didn't even make it to six months and within the short amount of time of him being there, things in my life began to die. Everything in my life was OFF. I mean, my praise was off. My prayer life was jacked-up. My money was even OFF because disobedience and sin in one area of your life has power to destroy other areas of your life, because ALL sins lead to death. But the one thing that was off and hurt me more than anything else, was my worship. I found myself in a position where I was unable to worship GOD and enter into HIS presence. Nothing in me was able to attend church Sunday after Sunday and lift Holy hands to a Holy God, knowing that my hands were unclean and that separation was unbearable. As much as I enjoyed him being there, I had to put that man out of my house because I knew that GOD was not pleased.

Beloved, GOD only corrects those that HE loves and it doesn't matter what kind of sin that you find yourself drowning in; shacking, fornicating, adultery, lying, gambling, homosexuality, stealing, slothfulness, or gossiping.

If you are a Christian and you are no longer being convicted by the Holy Ghost of your sin, then let this serve as a life-line to pull you back in because you are too far from GOD and I won't let you drown in that sin!

"...But where sin abounded, grace did much more abound" (Romans 5:20).

How Is Your Love Walk?

Over the last few years, a series of events have occurred in my life that have caused me to really examine myself. It's amazing how many of us will live most of our lives thinking and believing that we are something that we're not and we will inadvertently spend years moving and operating in those very things that we claim not to be. This goes for me as well. I never knew that I was selfish until I met a Man that was self-less. I never considered myself as being self-centered until I met a Man that was noble. I never thought that I was arrogant until I met a Man that was humble. I never knew that I was so guarded until I met a Man who was so transparent and the more time that I spent with this Man, the more I saw all that He was and He was love. He gave love, showed love and walked in love, and I don't mean man's interpretation of love. I mean 1 Corinthians 13:4-8 LOVE, which says:

"Love is patient and kind. Love is not jealous or boastful or proud or rude. It does not demand its own way. It is not irritable, and it keeps no record of being wronged. It does not rejoice about injustice but rejoices whenever the truth wins out. Love never gives up, never loses faith, is always hopeful, and endures through every circumstance" (NLT).

It was in this Man's presence that I saw all that I wasn't and all that I wanted to be. No, I wasn't a thief and no, I wasn't a liar. Yes, I was a woman of peace. Yes, I was polite and respectful. Yes, I was kind and generous, but my love walk was a bit shaky because in my own way, I could be a bit rude and truth be told - secretly, I kept a record of wrongs. So even though I could say "yes" and "no" to all of these other great qualities, I lacked the greatest quality of them all and that was love. If all that I am and if all that I do are not motivated and operated in love, then all that I do is in vain in the economy of GOD.

Therefore as a believer, I must always evaluate my love walk, because I don't care how anointed you are, how many crowds you can draw, what ministry you are on, how gifted you are and what title you carry - if you are not walking in love, then you are not walking with GOD, because GOD IS LOVE. He is not impressed by how many songs we can sing, how many books we can write, how many members are in our churches or how many letters are behind our names. He's impressed by our LOVE WALK.

So beloved, I challenge you today to ask yourself, "HOW IS YOUR LOVE WALK?" Because if fashion models can be zealous about their catwalks and people in the military can be obsessive about their cadence walk - then surely as Christians, we can be more passionate about our LOVE WALK.

HOW IS YOUR LOVE WALK?

"And walk in love, as Christ also hath loved us, and hath given himself for us an offering and a sacrifice to God for a sweet-smelling savor"
(Ephesians 5:2).

Are You Crippled?

Luke 13 speaks of a woman that was crippled by an evil spirit and for 18 years, that spirit held her in bondage and kept her bent over, unable to walk straight. It made me think how many DAUGHTERS OF ABRAHAM are actually bent over? Held in bondage by evil spirits? Crippled to the point where they are hunched over? Unable to walk straight? Unable to hold their heads up high because they have spiritual kyphosis? It makes me wonder how many of us are walking upright physically but internally, we are just as crippled as they come. We are crippled in our way of thinking. Crippled in our emotions. Crippled in our minds. Crippled in our souls. Crippled in our hearts. Crippled in our bodies. Crippled in our finances. Crippled in our relationships. Crippled in our lives.

KYPHOSIS is a disease of the spine that prevents a person from walking upright. It's a disease that prevents the spine from being able to carry the weight of the body and it doesn't allow the head to be balanced with the pelvis. Anytime a person's head does not have balance, they are bound to fall over. Many of us are falling over in many areas of our lives and are hunchbacked spiritually, because we are held in bondage and we don't even know it. But

DAUGHTER OF ABRAHAM, all it takes is one WORD and a TOUCH from JESUS and you too, can be free of your kyphosis.

"This dear woman, a daughter of Abraham, has been held in bondage by Satan for eighteen years. Isn't it right that she be released, even on the Sabbath?" (Luke 13:16 / NLT).

Do You Need Directions?

Many of us live our entire lives WITHOUT ANY DIRECTION. We live our lives on a TRIAL and ERROR basis; wandering around the same circle, butting up against the same issues, making the same mistakes, living in the same ball of confusion and never getting the victory, NEVER accomplishing anything significant. Then we link up with other people that have NO DIRECTION and it becomes a continuous cycle of the BLIND LEADING THE BLIND. BLIND PEOPLE do not know if they should be STRAIGHT OR GAY; if they should be SOBER or HIGH, if they should LIE or TELL THE TRUTH, if they should be SOULED OUT FOR JESUS or BALL for the DEVIL, if they should GAMBLE or TITHE, if they should MARRY HIM or LET HIM GO, if they should be HOT or COLD, if they should walk in FAITH or LUCK or if they should START THE BUSINESS or STAY ON THE JOB, etc. We constantly live in chaos, being up and down and tossed to and fro, because we don't do this one simple thing: ACKNOWLEDGE GOD.

"In all thy ways acknowledge HIM, and HE shall direct thy path"
(Proverbs 3:6).

~ If you acknowledge Him, you will get some direction for your life!~ #NoMoreWanderingInTheWilderness

Are You An Addict?

When we think of addictions we often think of people that are addicted to drugs, alcohol or cigarettes. We may also include sex and food in some of these obvious addictions, but when I think of addictions I think of something totally different. I was an addict on so many levels: and any time you find yourself so wrapped up and so hungry for a thing that you find it hard to focus on anything else, you are an addict.

In my younger years I would risk my life and my freedom for it, but as I got older I found other ways to get it and getting it became my life. I would work 50-70 hours a week just to possess it and the more of it I had, the more of it I wanted. It caused me my social life and many important family events that I'll never be able to get back again. It caused me my health and it drained me mentally, physically and spiritually - but I still wanted it more than anything. It caused me relationships with some really good men, because no man could come before it. Most of all, it caused me my relationship with GOD because you can't serve 'it' and GOD.

Without even realizing it, I had put it on the throne of my heart and made it my god, because NOTHING was more important to me than making MONEY. I lived to make money. I woke up to make money. It was the one thing that motivated me. I had all that I needed and even more of what I wanted. As long as I had money, life was good so I thought - until one day I noticed that fluid was leaking from my breast and immediately I started thinking about death. The doctor said I had a brain tumor and it was at that very moment when I realized that my MONEY could not help me. The one thing that I invested so much of my time getting, was the one thing that could help me the least. The one thing that I thought about night and day, was the last thing on my mind because money isn't an issue when life hits you with issues that money can't solve. There are some things in life that MONEY just can't buy.

Have You Really Divorced It?

It's amazing how we give DIVORCE DECREES, but we NEVER really leave. We stay attached. We still date it. We still answer to it. We still text it. We still give it our time. We still flirt with it. We still pacify it. We still give our money to it or take money from it. We still reach out to it when a need arises and no matter how bad it was or is for us, we still defend it. We still give it accolades and we still stay close enough to it to allow it to rule our lives. I'm convinced that many of us have issued DIVORCE DECREES to SPOUSES, PEOPLE and THINGS, but we can't leave a thing that we have become a SLAVE to spiritually, mentally and/or emotionally.

~ You may have issued the DECREE, but the DIVORCE isn't FINAL until your MIND gets FREE. ~

Can You Handle Your Kryptonite?

Kryptonite was the ultimate natural weakness of Superman and the word Kryptonite has since become synonymous to the one weakness of an otherwise invulnerable hero. I believe that we all have our kryptonite, with sin being the originator of most of them. Some people's KRYPTONITE may be alcohol and others may be men with full beards or bowed legs. But whatever it is, when confronted with a decision that may cause you to have to interact with it - be sure to ask yourself, "Can I work with my KRYPTONITE? Can I minister to someone that is my KRYPTONITE? Can I just inbox, text and call my KRYPTONITE? Can I do anything with my KRYPTONITE besides stay away from it, without it killing me?" If so, you are good because SUPERMAN never could.

Are You an Emotional Roller Coaster?

God never said, "*Walk in your emotions or your flesh.*" He said, "*WALK IN THE SPIRIT*". Many of us keep getting tricked up and living our lives on emotional roller coasters, simply because we are walking in the wrong thing. Therefore, we're being governed and ruled by the wrong things called feelings and emotions. "*If we live in the Spirit, let us also WALK IN THE SPIRIT*" (Galatians 5:25).

~ Aren't you tired of being UP and DOWN? Make this your last STOP on this RIDE. ~

Where Are You?

As I'm fresh into another year I'm already pumping my brakes and asking myself, "Where am I?" Not to imply that I am lost, but just to get a clear direction of where I am going. Often we have so many goals on our agendas at the beginning of the year, we find ourselves tackling everything at once; picking up a lot of tasks and by the time we get to the second quarter, we are off track and burnt out with little or nothing accomplished.

So before I do a repeat of previous years, I am popping the question in the beginning of the first quarter, "Phaedra, where art thou?" In the past, I've been known to pop the question at the beginning of the fourth quarter and by that time, I'm so far off course that it takes me the entire three months just to get back to my starting point. By that time, the year is over and there's no time left to accomplish anything significant because I allowed the little foxes to destroy my vine and my time. I allowed the distractions of life to do just that - avert me from my purpose. However, that won't happen this year because I refuse to waste another one, being tossed to and fro by the winds of life. This year, the winds of life are going to have to blow around me, because I'm standing firm and my mind is set in one direction - my purpose and destiny.

So as I locate myself, I challenge you to do the same by asking yourself the question, "Where are you right now?" Some of us are on Preparation Drive and that's good. Some of us entered this year on Prosperity Road and that's great. A few of us mustered up just enough strength to make it into the year on Tired Lane and some of us are struggling in our minds trying to make it off of Depressed Blvd - while others are on Pause Street just waiting for a go. If the truth be told, many of us are already on Confused Avenue trying to figure out how in the world did we get here so early in the year? A few of us have already hit dead ends and others have wisely begun to take detours. But no matter which road you find yourself on - ALWAYS be able to locate yourself because that's the key to being found and to getting yourself moving back in the right direction.

Adam/Eve, where art thou?

Chapter 4
You Glow Girl!

On the Potter's Wheel

The difference is some pieces of clay act like they NEVER did; but I will tell you what I did and what I didn't do, what I no longer do and what I still want to do, because I am still on the POTTER'S WHEEL.

"But now, O Lord, thou art our father; we are the clay, and thou our potter; and we all are the work of thy hand" (Isaiah 64:8).

Embrace Your Brilliance

LADIES, you NEVER have to compare yourself to another woman because just like each diamond has its own unique cut, color and clarity - God created each of us the same way. We have our own unique cut, color and clarity and no matter how much the next diamond may shine, it can NEVER decrease another diamond's weight or value, or take away from its brilliance. The same applies for you because you are wonderfully and fearfully made by the CHIEF DIAMOND CUTTER HIMSELF and in HIM, you have no FLAWS and you shine just right. #embraceyourbrilliance

Dig Deeper

There are wells inside of you that you have NOT tapped into yet, so you have to dig deeper than what you are digging!
~ NOTHING of real value is ever found on the surface. The oil is at the bottom of the well. ~
#DigDeeperN2YOURCREATIVITY

Keep Your Gown Clean!

Years later and I can still hear her voice saying, "Phaedra, you must keep your gown clean at all times for you never know the time or the hour that THE BRIDEGROOM is coming." So even when I get a little speck on my dress, I am rushing to get it off and thanking God that I haven't stained it because I don't want my dress to be dirty. I want HIM to find me clean, pure and holy when HE comes.
#sistakeepurgowncleanatallcost

Diamonds & Pearls

I know that the pressures of life are great right now and there's HEAT coming from every angle, but endure. God is making DIAMONDS and PEARLS out of you.

Go Ahead and Cry

God knows the language of tears and not one of your tears are able to fall without HIM catching it and recording it. So go on child and cry!
"You keep track of all my sorrows. You have collected all my tears in your bottle. You have recorded each one in your book"
(Psalm 56:8).

Growing Up!

A big part in growing up is recognizing who or what's slowing you up!
"Let us lay aside every weight, and the sin which doth so easily beset us," (Hebrews 12:1).

Rainbow

I saw a young lady in the store and she turned and said, "I didn't know that you shopped in RAINBOW?" I said, "I shop in the THRIFT STORE too." Your value isn't based on where you purchase your clothes. Your value is based on what God has placed inside of you. You make the clothes. The clothes don't make you.

.

The Giant Slayer

Don't focus on the "giant" in your life when the God we serve is a "GIANT SLAYER." Shift your focus and keep your eyes on Jesus and not on your situation.

Just Do It!

I know that your dream and vision are both bigger than you. I know that your circumstances are contrary to the promise right now and I know that the instructions that you were given don't seem to make any sense at all. But if He said it, "SHALL HE NOT MAKE IT GOOD?" Although you don't have all of the pieces to the puzzle and though you don't fully understand all that GOD is telling you to do, JUST DO IT ANYWAY because your obedience will be the very thing that brings about the manifestation of your miracle.

"His mother said to the servants, "Do whatever he tells you." Now there were six stone water jars there for the Jewish rites of purification, each holding twenty or thirty gallons. Jesus said to the servants, "Fill the jars with water." And they filled them up to the brim. 8 And he said to them, "Now draw some out and take it to the master of the feast." So they took it. When the master of the feast tasted the water now become wine, and did not know where it came from though the servants who had drawn the water knew, the master of the feast called the bridegroom 10 and said to him, "Everyone serves the good wine first, and when people have drunk freely, then the poor wine. But you have kept the good wine until now."

This, the first of his signs, Jesus did at Cana in Galilee, and manifested his glory. And his disciples believed in him" (John 2:5-11 ESV).

Drop It Like It's Hot!

Sometimes we get engaged and/or get married for all of the wrong reasons. Some people will get engaged to or marry the wrong person simply because they don't want to disappoint their families. Others will stay engaged to the wrong person because they already purchased or received a ring. Some will stay engaged and marry the wrong person because they've already invested money on a dress and other wedding expenses. Others will stay engaged or move forward with marrying the wrong person simply because they don't want to be embarrassed - but the reality is you have more to lose marrying the wrong person, than you ever would letting them go! #That'sNOTtheONE

Protect Your Virtue

Ladies, always remember that the enemy is a robber of virtue. So be forever mindful of the men that you allow into your space. Be forever mindful of the people that you link up with. Be forever mindful of the company that you keep. Be forever mindful of what you allow to enter into your ear gates and your eye gates. Be forever mindful of your attire and the signals that it sends. Be forever on guard to PROTECT YOUR VIRTUE.

Rubies Don't Have Nothing On You

Diamonds NEVER get taken off of the market for anything less than what they are worth and neither should you. You are more valuable than any precious stone. There's a ruby out there that is worth $18 billion dollars and God says that HIS DAUGHTERS are worth far more than that. *"Who can find a virtuous woman? For her price is far above rubies"* (Proverbs 31:10).

#Don'tSellYourselfShort

Meet Phaedra

Phaedra T. Anderson is a woman chasing the heart of God. She's an author, poet, massage therapist, Esthetician and aspiring business owner. She has made contributions to the Philadelphia Daily News, The Germantown Courier, Gospel4U Magazine, Beyond Magazine, Women of Significance Magazine, Motivateus.com and currently writes for BronzeMagonline.com. She is also a contributing author in the book <u>Walk in Your Purpose</u>, where her story "Developed in Darkness" will cause one to have faith - even in the most uncertain moments of their life.

Phaedra has been coined as a "Creative, Word-Smith" because she is not just your ordinary writer. This Philadelphia native has been writing since the tender age of eight years old and is very skillful with her usage of words. Her writing style has the unique ability to penetrate the hearts and minds of readers from all walks of life. She is passionate about teaching the younger generation of women valuable lessons about Godly living and womanhood; which she distinctly does with the use of parables, quotes and short stories. Her passion to teach this younger generation of women has landed her various interviews on radio and TV shows including, Gospel4U Network and A Different Spirit. Her desire to always be a bridge for someone is reflected in her work as she strives to uplift, encourage, challenge and edify her readers.

 Phaedra.Anderson@yahoo.com

 @Phaedra Anderson

 @Phaedra Millionairess Anderson

www.phaedraanderson.weebly.com

Made in the USA
Middletown, DE
24 April 2016